VOCAL SELECTIONS

FROM

"THE UNSINKABLE MOLLY BROWN"

By

MEREDITH WILLSON

WILMETTE PUBLIC LIBRARY
1242 WILMETTE AVENUE
WILMETTE, IL 60091
847-256-5025

Contents

FRANK MUSIC CORP. and MEREDITH WILLSON MUSIC

Exclusively Distributed By

HAL•LEONARD®
CORPORATION
7777 W. BLUEMOUND RD. P.O. BOX 13819 MILWAUKEE, WI 53213

I Ain't Down Yet

From the M.G.M. Motion Picture "The Unsinkable Molly Brown"

By
MEREDITH WILLSON

And if that house is red and has a big brass bed I'm liii - vin' there. Too Too Too

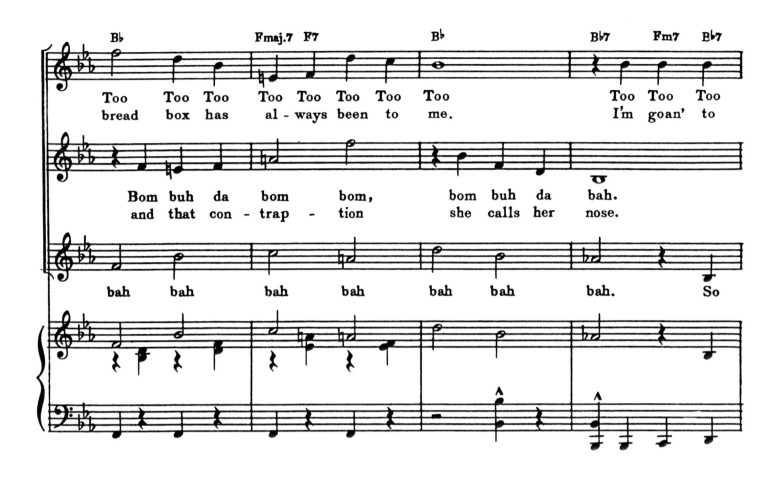

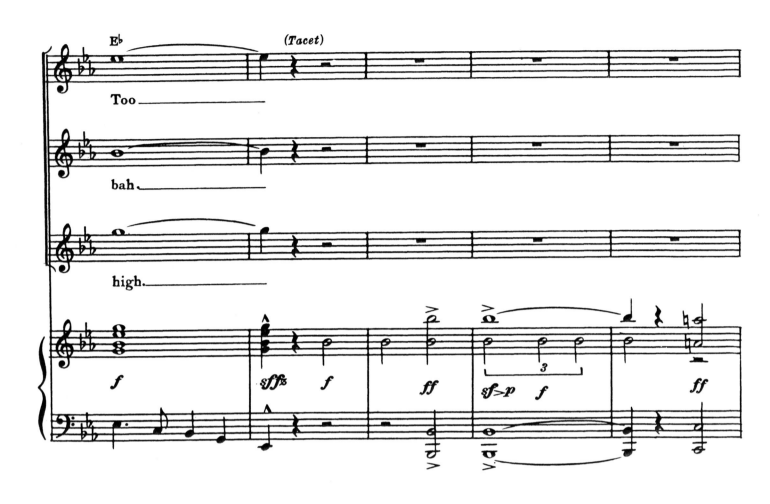

If I Knew

From the Broadway Musical "The Unsinkable Molly Brown"

By
MEREDITH WILLSON

sigh. Then I'd know how the ramb-lers bloom as they

do. And at last I'd know the se - cret of

you, of you, At last I'd know the se - cret of

1. you.

2. you.

Belly Up To The Bar, Boys

From the M.G.M. Motion Picture "The Unsinkable Molly Brown"

By
MEREDITH WILLSON

*Dolce Far Niente

From the M.G.M. Motion Picture "The Unsinkable Molly Brown"

By
MEREDITH WILLSON

*(Dol-che Far N-yen-teh)
"Sweet Nothings"

He's My Friend

From the M.G.M. Motion Picture "The Unsinkable Molly Brown"

By
MEREDITH WILLSON

Hoe Down Tempo

Verse

1. Tend-ing bar is a
2. Stand-ing there is a
3. Next to him is

man named Mor - gan. Sings in the choir and pumps the or - gan.
man named Flan-ni-gan. Got a good grip on a whale of a Bran-ni-gan.
Shor-ty Ban - nion. Saw me fall in-to Shirt-tail Can - yon.

Choose me and you got-ta choose Mor - gan, He'll come charg-in' in.
Choose me and you got-ta choose Flan-ni-gan, He'll come charg-in' in.
All-a-way home on the back of Ban - nion I come rid-in' in.

Refrain (after 1st, 2nd and 3rd Verses)

He's My Friend,___ and he'll stay my friend,___ Does-n't mat-ter what the oth-er peo-ple say.___

He's My Friend___ to the bit-ter end E-ven though the bit-ter end's a mil-lion years a-way.___

Verse

4. See that hob-ble on Sam-my Shee - han? Got it the night of the mass-a - cree - in'.
5. Wait-in' ta-ble's a gal named An-na-bel, Drinks like a fish and eats like a can-na-bel.
(Spoken) 6. To-ny or Hunk-y or an-y a' the rest of 'em, Airs pret-ty blue to the east or west of 'em.

Tom-a-hawk swung, I yelled "Shee - han!" He come charg-in' in.
'F I should hol-ler "Am-bush, An-na-bel!" She'd come charg-in' in.
Choose one from the worst or best of 'em And I'll come charg-in' in. Don't push him!

Refrain

(Tacet)   B♭ *(Tacet)*   E♭ *(Tacet)*

4. He's
5. She's My Friend_ and { he'll / she'll stay my friend_ Does-n't mat-ter what the
Sung: 6. He's   { he'll

Leadville Johnny Brown
(Soliloquy)

From the M.G.M. Motion Picture "The Unsinkable Molly Brown"

By
MEREDITH WILLSON

Spoken freely: This is my home, here. Leadville! Hell, that's my name, don't you know it?

Very Slowly

I just got one favor to ask you, Molly. We said goodbye, didn't we? All right.

Now just stay away! Don't you come back, ever! When I get ready to say goodbye, I say it and I go!

Moderately Slow

D♯dim   C   C♯dim   C♯m6   Dm7-5   Dm7   E7-5   E7

Remember, I said goodbye to Leadville, once? Well, I left, didn't I?

Am   Am7   B7   B7-5   E+7-9 E+7   E7

Sung: Said good-bye __ and walked a - way, _____ Walked a - way from

Colorado, My Home

From the M.G.M. Motion Picture "The Unsinkable Molly Brown"

By
MEREDITH WILLSON

Bon Jour
(The Language Song)
From the Broadway Musical "The Unsinkable Molly Brown"

By
MEREDITH WILLSON

"Chow." What-ev-er Jap-a-nese say while bow-ing low_

I mur-mur back "O - Hi - o"_ "Cal-lie Mer-ra"

greets_ the Greek and lets the sun-light trick-le right in. And if I

talk with an ac-cent, What's the dif-f'rence? A gr-in is a gr-in is a

I'll Never Say No

From the M.G.M. Motion Picture "The Unsinkable Molly Brown"

By
MEREDITH WILLSON